ONE MAN'S TRANSFORMATION
THROUGH THE POWER OF JESUS

and such were some of you

DANIEL O. MARTIN

HIS
4 EVER

Grove City, Ohio

AND SUCH WERE SOME OF YOU

Print: 979-8-9897188-0-1
E-book: 979-8-9897188-1-8

Book Design and cover illustration by TLC Book Design, *TLCBookDesign.com*
Cover by Tamara Dever; Interior by Erin Stark

Dedication

I WOULD LIKE TO DEDICATE THIS BOOK, FIRST AND foremost, to the Lord, without whom my journey would have never been possible.

Secondly, I would like to extend my appreciation to my mom and dad. Life has not always been easy, but they provided me with a great home where I learned about Jesus.

I would also like to thank the many people who have encouraged me along the way to write my story out for all to read. I struggled with this for quite some time, but I know God's hand is on this work. Thank you, brothers and sisters!

Table of Contents

Be blessed, encouraged,
challenged but most of all
rest in His Love
and accept His plan.
It is His will none perish.

2 PETER 3:9 PARAPHRASE

Introduction

I AM TRULY HONORED TO HAVE THE OPPORTUNITY to share my story with you about how Jesus has saved me and given me a true sense of worth, value, and hope in a world that provides none.

The title of this book has been taken from 1 Corinthians 6:11. It is the inspiration that provides me hope to this day and the title the Lord laid on my heart. There is hope for the homosexual, hope for the prostitute, and hope for the adulterer. Maybe you are reading this and saying that you have never been involved with any of the sins mentioned in this passage. That is alright. You still need Jesus. He is the only one who can bring hope, joy, and peace to a troubled soul. The cover was taken on my trip to Israel while visiting the ruins of a Roman city called Beit She'an. This city had a history of worshipping pagan gods. All types of sexual sin, including prostitution, ran rampant. Men and women alike were involved with the oldest profession during this time. What makes this picture so special to me is that the day we were visiting, this rainbow appeared. God can and will bring His hope and mercy to the darkest parts of our lives. There is no person or place that is not beyond His reach and touch. I can relate to Beit She'an. I was once there and know the shame of what my life had become. I also appreciate the rainbow representing the hope and love of God.

Before I share with you my life's journey, I must start by giving Him all of the glory and credit for what He has done in my life. All I did was take Him at His Word and believed. He did the rest. For so many years, I tried to pave my own way and make my own plan. You can see where it got me—right into the arms of my Lord. I tried to run from Him, but ended up running right into Him (Psalm 139:7-9). I have learned that my ways are a dead-end street, but His way is the only way.

Jesus said to him, "I am the way, the truth, and the life. No one comes to the Father except through Me."

JOHN 14:6

Some of my account may be difficult to read, and I have done all I can to tone down much of the content while not compromising my account. As you read, please remember God is a good God. The bad things that happened to me, He turned them around for good. He has never harmed me and has only sought to draw me in. If you are reading this book, I pray that the Lord's never-ending love for you will become real. He does love you more than I could possibly write or tell you in a conversation.

Every good gift and every perfect gift is from above, and comes down from the Father of lights, with whom there is no variation or shadow of turning.

JAMES 1:17

Be blessed, encouraged, and challenged,
but most of all, rest in His Love and accept His plan.
It is His will that none perish.

2 PETER 3:9 PARAPHRASE

For you did not receive the spirit of bondage again to fear, but you received the Spirit of adoption by whom we cry out, "Abba, Father."

ROMANS 8:15

Adoption—God's Plan

I WAS BORN ON SEPTEMBER 8, 1966, IN CLEVELAND, Ohio. My parents adopted me as an infant. When it was time for me to come home from the hospital after birth, I was taken directly to their home in Niles, Ohio. Before I go into my childhood, I would like to share with you my feelings on adoption and how it has not only impacted my life, but also given me life. I am forever grateful to my adopted (real) parents, who gave their lives to provide the best home possible. I really do not know where my life would have ended up without God's hand placing me in their care. The Lord trusted them to care for me and teach me about Him and His plan. That is exactly what they did throughout my childhood and into adulthood. To alleviate any confusion, I will refer to my adopted parents as Mom and Dad or my parents. There have been several times I have shared my story with close friends. When I mention my parents, often times, I need to explain who I am referring to. I only have one set of parents, but I am forever grateful to the people who birthed me. Additionally, I appreciate their unselfishness by realizing the need to place me in a home that could adequately provide for me and give me a future. I was able to meet with them in my early adulthood, but I will never see them as my parents.

I love how God's plan to draw us to Him is adoption (Ephesians 1:5; Romans 8:15). Without it, none of us would be eligible to become His child. When we give our lives to Him, we receive His Spirit and then have access to our Heavenly Father. He already paid the price for your salvation and adoption (John 3:16-17). However, we each must choose whether or not we will accept His perfect gift. God's perfect gift was delivered by His only begotten Son, Jesus Christ. If you have not yet accepted Jesus into your heart, I encourage you to. Ask Him to forgive you of your sins and come into your life. He will change you from the inside out and give you a reason and purpose to live. This world can only provide a temporal state of happiness, but Jesus will give you joy (John 15:11) and peace (Ephesians 2:14) that this world will not and cannot provide.

For you did not receive the spirit of bondage again to fear, but you received the Spirit of adoption *by whom we cry out, "Abba, Father."*

ROMANS 8:15, EMPHASIS MINE

Having predestined us to adoption *as sons by Jesus Christ to Himself, according to the good pleasure of His will.*

EPHESIANS 1:5, EMPHASIS MINE

For God so loved the world that He gave His only begotten Son, that whoever believes in Him should not perish but have everlasting life. For God did not send His Son into the world to condemn the world, but that the world through Him might be saved.

JOHN 3:16-17

"These things I have spoken to you, that My joy may remain in you, and that your joy may be full."

JOHN 15:11

For He Himself is our peace, who has made both one, and has broken down the middle wall of separation.

EPHESIANS 2:14

I was the oldest child of three in my family. My sister Rachel was born on June 20, 1969, roughly three years after I was born. We are not blood-related, and she had the same entrance into our family as I had. When she was able to come home from the hospital after birth, she came directly to her new home with us. I do not think in today's world, mothers are kept in the hospital after childbirth. In those days, it was the norm. Even though I was only three years old, I remember how cool it was to have a little sister.

Roughly two years after Rachel was born, Mom conceived and gave birth to our sister Rose. I had just started kindergarten when she was born. It was amazing that, within five years, there were now three of us. Wow, I now had two baby sisters! I remember that when my mom came home from the hospital with Rose, my dad had decorated our entire house with pennants. Mom always liked pennants. Every time we drove past a used-car dealership, she would comment on how pretty they were. Rose was a most welcome addition to our family. She brought joy and hope and was an answer to prayer. We were now a complete family, and everything was going well. I understand that Rose's birth was extra special to my parents, but this in no means detracted from the love they had for Rachel and I. While growing up, Mom and Dad never presented adoption in a negative sense. Rachel and I were never conditioned or made to feel we were less than their child because we were adopted. Additionally, our background was never a secret kept from us. When we were old enough to understand and started asking questions, they explained it to us. This openness my parents provided gave me a positive outlook on adoption and helped me to see God's plan as one of love. This aided me in years to come when I became very angry with God and wanted nothing to do with Him. Unfortunately, I had to walk down some dark roads that were the design of my own choices. It never changed the fact that God continually tried to get my attention.

I have never been a father, so I cannot understand firsthand what a blessing it must be to bring life by God's hand into this world. Jesus is referred to as "the author of life" (Acts 3:15 ESV), who gave and still gives "the breath of life" (Genesis 2:7). I want to encourage you that if you were adopted or born into a family, God has always been there for you, tugging on your heartstrings. He died so you could become a member of His family through Jesus. Maybe you feel that God just doesn't love you or have time for you. Maybe you have done things that make you feel bad. Nothing could be further from the truth. Even though He cannot tolerate sin, He died for you and paid the eternal penalty for your sins. Before I became a Christian and experienced His love and acceptance, I was heavily involved in many things that were bad. I was on a very fast road to hell, and the only exit sign I had was from Him. I was convinced that God could never love or accept me. He has totally forgiven me of my sin, and He will do the same for you. Give the author of life a chance. He will never let you down and never leave you (Hebrews 13:5; Joshua 1:9).

I love how the Psalms describe how intricately God is involved from our very beginning, before our birth. You may think that the passage I am about to share was only for the psalmist David. I assure you that God sees us all in this light. He is the only One who is able to know everything about everyone at any time. He is the ultimate Father.

I will praise You, for I am fearfully and wonderfully made;
Marvelous are Your works,
And that my soul knows very well.
My frame was not hidden from You,
When I was made in secret,
And skillfully wrought in the lowest parts of the earth.
Your eyes saw my substance, being yet unformed.
And in Your book they all were written,
The days fashioned for me,
When as yet there were none of them.
How precious also are Your thoughts to me, O God!
How great is the sum of them!

*If I should count them, they would be more in number
than the sand;
When I awake, I am still with You.*

PSALM 139:14-18

I apologize for getting off subject, but God's Word has transformed me. Since this book is about His work and not mine, I must include His Word. Let me get back on track.

Although all had been going well, our family soon faced tragedy and great loss. One afternoon, on a cold January morning, my aunt Betty stopped and picked me up at Garfield Elementary. I was five years old and in kindergarten. I do not remember her telling me why she came to get me, though she may have mentioned that she was taking me home. I do not remember much of the scene when I got home, but my parents were very sad. We had lost Rose to Sudden Infant Death Syndrome (SIDS) the night before. Rachel and I were too young to grasp what had happened, but we knew Rose had been taken to be with Jesus in heaven. I remember asking my mother if an angel was in our house that night. That is my most profound memory of the loss of my sister.

My memory is vague since I was only five years old. Even though Rose Elizabeth Martin only lived for two months, she brought joy to our family. I anticipate the day I will see her again in heaven. Despite being crushed by this tragedy, my parents never ceased to provide a safe, loving home for Rachel and I. My parents are both Christians, and I was raised in the church. I know what got them through this was their faith in God and love for each other and us. Even though I was raised with the knowledge of salvation and God's love for me, I did not give my life to Him until well into my adult years. I will go into more details of my conversion later in this book. Looking back on my life, even though I lived so long without Him in my heart, He has been faithful.

God has a special place in His heart for all children and wants them to have a loving, caring home. Adoption is a choice that definitely gave Rachel, me, and many others a chance in life. The Lord knew exactly where to place us to give us what we needed for life. The framework for adoption mirrors God's plan for mankind. Without adoption, none of us would have a chance to become His child.

Then little children were brought to Him that He might put His hands on them and pray, but the disciples rebuked them. But Jesus said, "Let the little children come to Me, and do not forbid them; for of such is the kingdom of heaven."

MATTHEW 19:13-14

When Jesus came from heaven as a baby, He had you in mind. The only way any of us would have a chance to spend eternity with Him and be forgiven of all of our sins was if He stepped in and made a way for us. He became our bridge to the Father, a bridge that humanity could not design or build. It is tremendously comforting to know that Jesus loved me and you enough to leave heaven to give us an opportunity to be adopted into His family. This is the greatest act of love anyone could do.

When He died on the cross and rose again, He afforded us all the option to choose. We can either choose Him and be a part of His family (His Church). The other option is to continue to serve ourselves (Deuteronomy 30:19). I realize that may sound very judgmental; however, this is His plan, not mankind's. Many times, when I was not yet serving Jesus, I would get very upset when a close-minded Christian would say there was only one way—Jesus (John 14:6). I would go out of my way to challenge them and tell them they were wrong. I had experienced so many hurts at the hands of others that I could not get past the many hurdles of how I perceived God's people. My cloudy view of Christians also affected how I saw God. I cannot give an explanation on why and how certain things have happened to me, but I do know that while I was a sinner, He died for me and looked after me (Romans 5:8). He is looking after you as well. If you haven't received Him as your Savior, I encourage you to ask Him to reveal His great love for you. He will never let you down. He will always accept you as you are. Yes, He does want to change you, but not to steal from you. He wants to exchange your brokenness for His new life. There is a new life in Him waiting for you. The price has been paid, but the decision is yours. If you are a Christian and reading this book, I encourage you to reach out with the love of Jesus to those who need Him.

*"I call heaven and earth as witnesses today against you,
that I have set before you life and death,*

blessing and cursing; therefore choose life,
that both you and your descendants may live."

DEUTERONOMY 30:19

Thomas said to Him, "Lord, we do not know where You are
going, and how can we know the way?" Jesus said to him,
"I am the way, the truth, and the life.
No one comes to the Father except through Me."

JOHN 14:5-6

But God demonstrates His own love toward us, in that while
we were still sinners, Christ died for us.

ROMANS 5:8

This book is my story about how Jesus transformed me. I wanted the first chapter to be dedicated to the beauty of adoption, since it set the framework for the start of my life. If you are a parent, I want to thank you for the tough job you do. Like I said earlier, I have never fathered a child, but I realize it must be difficult yet rewarding. The Lord has entrusted you greatly with your children. That is a pretty honoring endorsement. God bless.

Adoption is God's blueprint
for humanity.
His design is perfect.
He loves us that much!

Early Childhood

FOR THE FIRST TWELVE YEARS OF MY LIFE, WE LIVED in Niles, Ohio, where I attended Garfield Elementary. My school was roughly one to two miles from my house, and I walked every day up to finishing the sixth grade.

This was the early 1970s, when it was still safe to walk to school as a young child. The threat of people opening car doors and coaxing children into cars was never an issue. Fortunately, I had cousins who also attended Garfield and lived on the way to school. Until they moved, I walked with them. Since they were older, they assured my safe passage. One time, I mentioned to them as we were walking to school that I did not want to walk with girls. Later on, I probably told them that I would walk with them. I realize that seems ironic considering the turns my life took later on; however, I was simply a headstrong first or second grader. I still remember them letting me walk ahead of them, not to strip me of my independence. It was all good, and I appreciated their company and the safety in numbers. I was too young to understand many of the dangers that an adult would. Nonetheless, the setup was good for me.

Since most of my cousins were girls, they were also (you guessed it) my primary babysitters. When I was very young, my parents would go out quite often and leave us in the care of either Renee, Carol, or Pam. I do not remember a lot of the details about their care except that they watched Rachel and me often. My parents were very happy with how they cared for us. To say my mom and dad went out often should probably be explained. They never went out drinking or were irresponsible. A lot of their outings were for choir, church functions, or dinner with friends or family. My biggest memory of my cousin babysitters was with my cousin Pam. I remember clear as day one night, when it was time to go to bed, I did not want to. She asked me why, and I told her I was afraid of the dark. She let me sleep downstairs and probably told my parents that she was reading me a book so I would not be in any trouble. The truth is, I was much afraid of the dark as a young child. I would sleep with a bed full of stuffed animals with the covers over my eyes. I was probably a sight to see. Fortunately, I outgrew this fear as I developed.

Another great benefit of walking to school was my grandparents (Dad's parents) lived on the way. I loved stopping by their house on the way to or from school. Sometimes, my cousins and I would stop by unannounced, and they would always welcome us with open arms and a sandwich, cookies, or anything else that might spoil our dinner. Grandma and Grandpa were like my parents, only cool. Like many grandparents, they spoiled us and loved us all in one. Grandpa and Grandma Martin seemed like the most prepared people in the world. My grandfather was an avid gardener. He had retired from the railroad and had the most beautiful flower garden. It was always perfect and well kept. He also had a snake. I did not like snakes, but he kept "Jake" in the back penned up. I'm not sure how you pen up a snake, but my grandfather did. Grandpa would go camping and canoeing and talk with me about the Bible and God. I can tell you one memory of him that all of his grandchildren have treasured. He had an office in his house. We were never allowed there unless he invited us. When he did, that was a treat. He had a stash of pink candies kept up high. Those candies are still available if you go to a store that sells the old-style candies. They were so good, but the best part was that they were from my grandfather. My grandmother never worked outside of the home, to my knowledge, but she could run a house like nobody's business. She raised a big family and easily had three times a return with the grandchildren. There was always food in her house, and she was always prepared to make a sandwich, soup, or whatever was needed. Many times after church, it was nothing for ten or so of us to stop by. She would get out all the fixings for bologna sandwiches and have enough for us all. My grandmother was also an avid canner. She made the best jams and jellies, which she kept in her basement. All of my memories of my grandparents are from my early childhood. I think those memories are the most innocent, never clouded with hang-ups that we often develop in our adult years.

Anyway, I was talking about walking to school and how it was beneficial to have my grandparents two blocks away on the way to school. It is very easy to get sidetracked when I am collecting my thoughts. Since my grandparents were both very talented with gardening and canning and lived on the way to and from Garfield Elementary, I regularly dropped in to get either flowers for my teacher or fresh jelly for my mom. They never complained or asked me, "Why are you stopping now?" They were always very loving and patient with all their grandchildren. I remember one day, en route to school, I stopped by their house and walked right in. It was early morning, and they were still in bed. My cousins had already moved to the other side of Niles, so I was alone. I remember going to the door of their bedroom and calling out to them. We were never allowed in their bedroom, especially when they were asleep. I announced that I needed some flowers for my teacher. There was no movement, but I heard Grandma say, "Ollie, go get the boy some flowers." He got up and cut me some fresh flowers and sent me on my way. They probably laughed after they woke up but were probably also happy they were able to not only bring joy to me, but also to my teacher. That was going to school. On the way home, I would stop and get homemade jelly. Grandma, not always, but on certain visits, would take me down to the basement and let me pick my own jar of jelly. This was a grade schooler's dream. Little did I know they were all the same, but she made me feel important. They always made everyone feel important and loved. They never treated me as their adopted grandson. I was their grandson. My grandparents served God, and every memory I have of them points to their commitment to Jesus. They were able to love the way they did because He lived inside of them. My grandfather was an avid reader of the Bible. He was an active teacher at our church and wrote a book—*A Study in the Revelation,* by Oliver S. Martin. I have been fortunate to have a copy of his book and have read it.

Living in town was really cool, but I did miss the wide-open spaces of the country that the neighborhood just could not deliver. Fortunately, I had cousins who lived on a farm with over one hundred acres. They had the big farm house, red barn, and plenty of hay and animals. It was always a great pleasure to get to visit my cousin Herman. He was my age, and we had a blast together. Whether we were playing in the hay in the barn, feeding the pigs, or milking the cows, every visit was an adventure. My uncle (Herman's father) was not only a farmer but also an over-the-road truck driver. He owned his own rig, so getting to see one of those was enough to keep this grade schooler mesmerized for an entire afternoon. We got into everything and had a blast. In fact, getting into everything got us into a lot of trouble on one visit. I don't know what we were thinking, but for some reason, we decided it would be fun and sporting to break all of the windows out of my uncle's big red barn. There were plenty of glass windows, the key word being were. To make matters worse, I decided it would be the best thing to tell my uncle we had done this. He was very upset. We both got grounded and spanked. I think the worse part of this was being grounded from seeing each other. The farm offered an environment I could not have, and I was closer to my cousin than anyone on Wyoming Avenue in Niles. We eventually served our time from the sentence handed down, but we never did anything that stupid ever again. We had both learned our lesson. That was a hard lesson for two five-year-old boys.

Of course, no young boy's childhood would be complete without pets. My dad was a mailman with the Postal Service. One day, he bought home a black cat. She was very young, and I immediately loved her. We named her "Puff." Puff turned out to be a handful and more trouble than she was worth. We had a very large oak tree in our front yard, and one day, Puff decided to climb it and could not get down. This was in the days when the fire department would come to the rescue, and they did. The Niles Fire Department made two trips to our home on Wyoming Avenue to rescue Puff from the clutches of the same tree. After the second time, she was never the same. She started acting strange, like pooping in my dad's shoe. One day, she took a swipe at my sister, and I smacked her across the room. We ended up taking her to my aunt's house in the country, where she learned to chase and catch mice. That was the end for her at our home. We also had a dachshund named "Tippy." I do not remember where she came from, but we got her as a puppy. I loved her very much. She had a special place in our family for years. She did give birth, and my grandfather, who had the wonderful garden, became the proud owner of her puppy "Flippy." The last pet I remember was a guinea pig named "Scooby Doo." I do not know if you have ever had a guinea pig, but they make the loudest, most annoying sound that goes right through you. Cousin Pam wasn't happy to come over and babysit once we got Scooby Doo, but she still did. Dad designed and built a cage for Scooby

Doo. The frame was designed to come out so we could place it in the yard for her to graze. One day, we put her out in the yard to eat grass within the safe confines of her cage. We had placed her in the shade, but as we all know, what is shaded in the morning is not in the afternoon. We forgot all about Scooby Doo. She survived, but it took her awhile to get back to making those horrible sounds only she could. I think Pam was happy, and babysitting became a pleasure once again—just kidding. The only other thing about guinea pigs is that they have to have wood chips in their pen so they can do their business. We would go to the mill on the other side of Niles, and my mom would get wood chips for Scooby Doo's pen, probably free of charge. I do not remember how she died, except she was there one day and gone the next. I realize that sounds brash, but I am speaking out of the memory of a young boy. These were our pets while in Niles. The only one that made the move was Tippy, the wiener dog—see the next chapter.

I enjoyed living in Niles. We lived close to most of our extended family, and you did not have to travel far to get to stores, parks, or movie theaters. I liked attending Garfield. There were many things and people at that school that made an impact on my very young life. My favorite teacher was Mrs. Vandergriff. I believe she was my fifth-grade teacher, but I am not sure. What made her special was that she genuinely cared about her students, and she liked me. She would tell our class about her pet monkey. This was very fascinating since all we had were dogs. Oh, we loved our dogs, and they were members of our family, but to have a pet monkey blew my little mind. She was a very kind and loving teacher. I will never forget that. I only wish some of my other teachers had been half as nice as her. I did have some really good, caring teachers while I was a student, but none compared to Mrs. Vandergriff.

Garfield Elementary was where I learned how to play the trumpet. I was in the school band, which comprised of only a few students. Since my parents wanted me to excel, I was also enrolled in private trumpet lessons at the local music store by the Eastwood Mall on the strip in Niles. The worst part of learning to play in the band was I had to carry that trumpet everywhere. When I walked home from school, I had it in tow. When we went to private trumpet lessons, I had it in tow. I know that seems awfully dramatic, but for a grade schooler, it seemed big. One day, while playing in the band, something happened. I do not remember if I got into trouble with the band director, but something happened or was said to me that was upsetting. I also do not remember how Mrs. Vandegriff found out what had happened, but she went down two flights of steps and gave the band director a piece of her mind. She was not only an amazing teacher, but also very protective of her students. What made this incident stick out in my memory was that Mrs. Vandegriff was very overweight. It was difficult for her to go up and down stairs. She did not let that get in her way, and, to this day, at age fifty-seven, I still remember her unselfishness and commitment to me that day. Thank you, Mrs. Vandegriff!

The only other memories I have of attending Garfield were passing out in my mashed potatoes and peeing my pants on the way to school. As far as the mashed-potato incident, it was winter, and we had just come in from recess for lunch. When I sat down with my tray, it was all I could do, and I went nose first into my mashed potatoes. As far as peeing my pants on the way to school, the walk was just too much for my little bladder. Hey, it happens. Fortunately, Mom came and rescued me.

There were certain scheduled daily and weekly events that we had to attend—school and church. I remember when I was in kindergarten, I was sick, but since it was picture day, I had to wear the ugliest shirt I owned and head to school. I don't remember anything about this particular day except that going to school in this ugly shirt was the last thing I wanted to do. The other mandated appointment was church. Our family, including extended family, attended Faith Baptist Church. Attending church was not a bad experience. I attended Sunday school in the church basement, and they always had juice and cookies. I learned about Jesus, and we sang a whole lot of songs. To this day, I can still remember a few. "Jesus Loves Me" will always stick with me.

After Sunday school, we would attend the church service in the main sanctuary. I had plenty of cousins in the church, and we all wanted to sit with Grandma and Grandpa. Looking back, it is quite humorous to think about all of us grandchildren sitting with our grandparents while our parents sat alone. I guess that is the way it is. Not that we didn't want to sit with our parents, but our grandparents were cool. Church also opened the door for me to experience church camp. Our church was affiliated with a camp called Stony Glenn. This place was amazing. There were plenty of hiking trails and things to do and see. This camp also had an outlook post overlooking the gorge. At the bottom of the gorge was the Grand River. Yes, we hiked down the gorge to the river. What group of grade school boys wouldn't want to take it all the way to see what was at the bottom? It was a rough hike, but our young, able bodies were up to the challenge. I'm not sure how our leader faired, but I never remember losing a fellow camper or counselor. The Grand River was full of mussels. If you have never seen or heard of a mussel, they are very similar to clams. We would catch them and then return them. It was all about sport, adventure, and fun.

I was also a member of a group called Awana. I attended this group at a different church (First Baptist). We still attended Faith Baptist, but I was allowed to be a part of this group. One of my friends, who lived a block from our house, went to this church, so I was able to get into the group because of him. This was the first group that boys and girls were together as one. We had to wear a uniform, which was really just a shirt with patches on it and blue jeans. They did a lot of cool things in this group. Awana sponsored a pinewood derby race. If you have never seen this, it is quite interesting and very fun. The church provided us each a pinewood derby kit to make our own racer. The kit contained a block of wood roughly twelve inches long, wheels, and a few other pieces of wood for the axels. We (actually, my dad) had to create our own car. The car could not weigh any more than a specified amount, and there were other restrictions that my dad had to consider when he helped me build and design mine. Dad was very smart and resourceful. He soldered metal on the bottom of my car, just coming in under the maximum weight. My car was yellow and blue and moved enough to get me first place. I had never won anything like that in my life. The *Niles Daily Times* took our picture and did an article on the race. This was so awesome.

Not only was I involved with Awana, but I was also a Cub Scout. Mom was the den mother and always had a way of keeping her pack of young boys busy so we would not get into trouble. The only memory I have of Cub Scouts is during one of our meetings. We were in my basement, and it was raining something fierce. Our basement had a tendency to leak really bad. This day was like no other. The walls burst like a dam, and our Cub Scout meeting was flooded. Thank God we had a drain in the floor, and the water could escape. In those days, no one let these types of setbacks steal the show. We continued with our meeting, and that was that. We were true grade school survivors.

Our family lived in Niles long enough for me to finish the sixth grade. Life up to this point was still pretty normal. I was too young to understand the feelings and yearnings that I would soon feel and experience going into my teen years. My parents decided to sell their house and build on my grand-mother's land near Columbiana, Ohio. My parents, especially my mom, had been through so much in that house with losing Rose. She has told me several times that she just didn't see the house the same after Rose's passing. I did not understand that then, but after experiencing loss later on in my life, it makes perfect sense and is fully understandable.

3

Teen Years

MY MOTHER'S FAMILY WAS NOT FROM NILES. SHE grew up in a rural area on the other side of the outskirts of Youngstown in Columbiana, Ohio. My grandmother owned over one hundred acres of land. She had provided my parents with five acres on the old Culp homestead for us to build a house. This was very exciting since it was new and a welcome change. My parents sold our house, and we moved. As fate would have it, our house was not completed by the time we had to move. Since my parents were very resourceful, they decided to buy a camper, and we lived in our driveway until the house was ready to move in. With the four of us, the camper was cramped, but we made it work, and all was well. All our belongings had to be put into storage. Our new home had yet to be carpeted when we moved in.

This happened quickly. Our new life was in the southernmost part of Mahoning County. I started school at South Range Middle School in the seventh grade. Going to school at South Range was much different than I had grown accustomed to in Niles. In Niles, I had to walk; here, I rode a bus, which seemed to take an eternity. The bus route I was on ran the perimeter of the school district, just grazing the next county. We hit every bump the country roads had to offer. My new school was much smaller than the Niles City Schools. One of the major differences in our new location was you needed a car to go anywhere. In Niles, I could walk or ride my bike and be where I was going in a relatively short amount of time.

Rachel and I soon adapted. We started to make friends, became involved in our new local church, and became members of 4-H. I traded in Awana and Cub Scouts for membership in the Eager Beavers. The 4-H club played a huge part of my childhood. Our group always had a booth at the Canfield Fair. This was the highlight for all the 4-H organizations. We would decorate our space at the fair to reflect our accomplishments and contributions to our community. Over the course of my involvement with 4-H, I showed bunnies and a goat. This was an honor, even though I never won a ribbon. The experience and thrill of showing my animals at the fair was enough for me.

The Canfield Fair (officially the Mahoning County Fair) was the main annual event in the Youngstown area. This was my mother's old stomping grounds. She showed us the animals, especially the draft horses. When her father was a farmer, he used draft horses to plow the fields and help with the heavy work of running a farm back in the forties. The Canfield Fair was an important part of Mom's childhood, and now, she was able to pass the experience on to us. In high school, I joined the marching band. We participated in band day, where all the county bands would play at the grandstands for the fairgoers. That was fun, even though we had to watch for horse drop-pings since we marched on the horse racing track. Even though it was a bummer to step in horse poop, we had a great time and made many fond memories. To this day, my parents still go to the fair and spend the day. I usu-ally accompany them, but they attend regardless. They are both in their mid-eighties and still going strong. I am very proud of them!

I mentioned I started the seventh grade at South Range Middle School. Middle school was a far cry from Garfield Elementary. I started to change as I entered my early teens. At the time, I thought much of the changes in my life were a result of the move. Don't get me wrong, they were. There was a definite adjustment for my fam-ily. As I developed, other changes surfaced. I started to notice boys, not girls.

Making friends at my new school seemed to be more difficult than it had been in Niles. I was the new kid in the school, and this awkward time in my development did not make my transition any easier. I was really skinny, wore glasses, and developed a bad case of acne. All of which were hard on a kid, especially a new one. I did make some new friends, most of whom were in the band. I played trumpet and sang in the choir. One thing that was really neat was that I learned how to march. The band director did this for everyone in the band to prepare us for high school, where we would be in the marching band and play at football games, band shows, and, of course, the Canfield Fair. I made it through the two years of middle school and was off to attend South Range High School, where I would once again be the new kid.

When I started the ninth grade, I was definitely in an awkward stage in my development. My high school years brought many changes, like it does with any high schooler. I learned how to drive and got my license. This opened up many doors for me, like working on the weekend and some nights after school. I worked at a fast-food restaurant for a while, then at a family restaurant. I was a dishwasher and did other odd jobs as needed. I really did not enjoy working in the restaurant, but that was what most of us did when awarded with a driver's license. My working career in high school did not last long, and I was really glad when it came to an end. The only other job I had while in high school was working for a friend's father, who owned a chinchilla and guinea pig farm. I worked in the lower level of the barn where the guinea pigs were. The animals were kept in several pens. My job was to clean their cages and discard any dead ones. It was messy, smelly, and difficult, but I was happier with this task then I was at washing dishes in the restaurant. I did this up to the end of high school. I also worked at the Canfield Fair during fair time at the ice cream stand.

High School was another rough four years. I never felt a part of anything, although I was a member of the band and chorus. I did have some friends, but I always felt like the odd ball out. This was when I first started noticing that I was different than most boys my age. I did not have same-sex attractions until later on, but I did notice I was not interested in girls.

When I entered the ninth grade, we had lived in Columbiana for roughly two years. My parents hosted every family meal for both her side (Culp) and his side (Martin). She entertained for Easter, Memorial Day, Labor Day, Thanksgiving, and Christmas. The largest, and I believe the most cherished and enjoyed gathering, was Labor Day. This annual event (one for each family) was dubbed "the Corn Roast." It was a great way to celebrate the end of summer and always happened at the same time as the Canfield Fair. This combination always attracted out-of-town family, so the attendance was always high. Of course, there was corn at the Corn Roast, but it was not roasted. My dad would boil it over an open firepit, and everyone who attended would bring a covered dish. We always had more than enough food and ate leftovers for some time afterwards. My parents always welcomed everyone.

Moving affected every part of our lives. Columbiana was approximately twenty miles from Niles. This was too far to go to church at Faith Baptist, where I had been raised. I'm not sure how my parents found Old North Baptist Church in Canfield, but that was where we landed. This church was much different from Faith Baptist. It was larger, and the environment was different. My transition from adolescent to teen was in overdrive, and I was experiencing many changes, not only in my body, but in the way I thought. I never felt a part of this church, but we were made to attend and be a part of church activities. It was expected. This church did not have an Awana, no pinewood derby, or larger-than-life banana split. I was not accepted by the other kids in my age group. I was new, and kids can be very mean, and some were. Many of them were not, but when you are young, new, and feel alone, the ones who are cruel seem to resonate with your mind. I will never forget our youth pastor, Randy. I really enjoyed talking with him. He truly cared about all of the youth in our church. I remember one summer, we all jumped in the church van and went up to Cadillac, Michigan, for a trip. Randy and his family had come to our church from Michigan. We all had a blast and were able to enjoy the beauty of Michigan. This was either the first, or one of the first, times I water-skied. These were the times at Old North that I cherished and enjoyed. Of course, I never enjoyed the cruelty of some of the youth, but people are not perfect, and their treatment is by no means how God is towards us.

In the introduction, I mentioned to remember that God is good as you read. Not only is He good, everything that has happened to me and you, He will turn it around for His glory. I hope you do not get the impression that I am painting God out to be a miser that is bent on benefiting from our hurts. That is by no means what my message is. He has not only used my pain for His glory, but He has also healed me and given me a life I could never have outside of Him. I am grateful to Him. I mention this now because I am about to write one of the most difficult portions of this book. I am doing so because someone needs to hear this, and I hope after reading this you will know God loves you and is calling you to Himself.

Our church had a camp (not Stony Glenn) in Northeast Ohio that the church youth attended for one week out of every summer. Your week was specific to your age group. There was plenty to do. I made new friends and got to swim, hike, and do arts and crafts. One summer, I applied to work at the camp the entire summer. For the first time in my life, I had to wash my clothes and operate without my parents in my day-to-day life. As an adult, an entire summer does not last that long, but when you are young, it seems like an eternity. I did make new friends, and for the most part, the time was well spent. This is where everything that seemed well-spent turned into one of the biggest tragedies of my life. One of my new friends, or so I thought, was an older camp worker. I will not mention his name, but he was in his late twenties, much older than my thirteen or fourteen years. We became friends, and he initially became like a big brother to me. He would talk to me and share stories from his life. I finally made a friend that seemed to care about me and have an interest in my well-being. As I got to know him more, I soon experienced another side of him that I never wanted, invited, and definitely did not bargain for. He molested me repeatedly over much of the course of the summer. I was so confused and lost I did not know where to turn or who to turn to. After this happened several times, I called my parents in tears. I felt so dirty and used but did not know how to handle these emotions and feelings.

My parents came up and met with me, and all I could do was cry. I could not bring myself to tell them what had happened. The shame I felt at the hands of this man ran very deep, very quickly. I was afraid no one would believe me. Before my parents came up, the camp director told me not to say anything to them, that the man who did this to me had been through a lot. Since I was swimming in shame and guilt, I did not mention this to my parents. When they arrived, they knew something really bad had happened, but I did not tell them, and they did not press me. The worst part of their visit was that they left me at the camp. I reclused deeper into my shame and realized that maybe I was meant to be an object for this man. The abuse continued throughout the summer. I never heard from him after I left the camp. The scars of these experiences ran deep. I had been violated! My parents had left me to fend for myself, and I felt abandoned by them. I became very angry with God and believed that I was a disposable entity to Him. How could He let this happen? How could He not have my parents protect me? How could He permit it to go on? Why did this happen at a church camp? I was taught that God was against homosexuality, so why did this happen to me in this environment? Why was I left with the deep wound in my heart that was so painful that I couldn't even be honest with myself? I was maybe thirteen and forced to carry the burden of these encounters all by myself. The aftermath of this atomic bomb forever changed my life and how I later approached relationships with others, mainly men.

Even though all of this happened and as angry as I was with God, He was still faithful to me. This truth would not become a reality until much later in my life. I had many years ahead of me that would be difficult. Everything was an uphill battle. By God's grace and divine protection, I made it through the impossible times. I would not make Jesus my Lord and Savior until many years later while in the Air Force. I will speak of my conversion and experience in the next chapter.

I graduated from high school in 1984 and enlisted in the US Air Force. I was on delayed enlistment since the job I had applied for in the Air Force was backed up. So, I did not leave for basic training until January 1985.

But God demonstrates
His own love toward us,
in that while we were
still sinners,
Christ died for us.

ROMANS 5:8

4

Young Adulthood

I'LL NEVER FORGET SITTING IN CLEVELAND HOP-
kins Airport on January 24, 1985, where a small group of
us from Northeast Ohio started our journey to Lackland
Air Force Base for basic training. We were all on the same
flight with the same problems and hurdles. Our biggest
problem was that we were snowed in and stuck in Cleveland. As I remember, the weather in Texas was much colder
than it usually was in January, but at least there was no
snow in San Antonio, the host city for Lackland Air Force
Base. I was eighteen years old and thought I was going on
vacation. Boy, did I get a rude awakening! Our flight eventually left Cleveland, and since we were so late leaving, we
missed our connecting flight in Houston. This was my first
time flying, and the bad weather made it an unpleasant
experience. We eventually made it to San Antonio and
arrived at Lackland Air Force Base. I'll never forget when
we got there, we were not welcomed with a smile and hot
chocolate. We were ordered to stand at attention until
the drill sergeant acknowledged us and gave us further
instruction. When he did come out, he made us pick up
our suitcases over our heads and put them back down mul-
tiple times. I guess this was to punish those of us, like me,

who packed a swimming suit, sunscreen, and everything else one would take on vacation.

When I enlisted in the Air Force, I was seventeen years old. My parents had to sign a waiver for them to accept me since I was still underage. I did not know why I enlisted except that I was promised opportunities to travel and see the world. I did not know who I was, and in many ways, I was running away from my problems and troubles. I was too young to realize I was attracted to men and did not accept those urges. I felt so much shame still due to the sexual abuse that I experienced several years prior at summer camp. I was not able to make any connections as to why I felt the way I did. All I knew was that my grades were not good enough to get into college, and I did not want to stick around home any longer. It was time for me to leave, and this was the only way I could get out of Dodge. I was not angry with my parents, but I still resented their lack of protection against a monster that should have been stopped, arrested, and made to pay for what he did to me. I did not trust men.

Although I was starting to feel drawn to men, I could not trust them because of the abuser and the male role models in my life who did not come to my rescue when I needed them most. More deeply embedded in my mind and heart was that I believed God did not care for me. How could He let this happen? Why did He let this happen? Would He ever make good and at least be honest with me about how He felt about me? I never wanted to believe that God did not love me, but I did. So, I did the only thing I knew, and it was not conscious. My human nature went into fight-or-flight mode. I went into flight and joined the US Air Force. The problem was when I ran from my problems, I ended up taking them with me. At eighteen years of age, I already had a few carry-ons, check-ins, and steamer trunks. No child should ever have to carry this type of weight, but I did. With these dynamics already in place in my very young life, I was set up to make more bad decisions, one after the other.

The enemy used these dynamics as a foundation to set me up to make more bad choices. I am forever grateful that God is more powerful than the enemy. Jesus was with me every step of the way. Through every bad decision and pit that I dug for myself, He was always there, and He is there for you as well.

But God demonstrates His own love toward us,
in that while we were still sinners, Christ died for us.

ROMANS 5:8

I graduated basic training then went to technical school at Keesler Air Force Base in Biloxi, Mississippi, where I spent the next six weeks learning my new trade—administration.

When I graduated from technical school, I landed at Holloman Air Force Base, southwest of Alamogordo, New Mexico. This was my first assignment in the Air Force, and it was very exciting. Of course, I wanted to either be in California or Florida, so they accommodated me by sending me to New Mexico (at least I got the sand of the beach). At this time, everything was new. I was very young and impressionable. I learned so much about the military and was starting to transition more into adulthood despite still being in my late teens.

I made friends and started attending church. The church I attended was much different than the Baptist church I had grown up in. Here, people raised their hands in church and were much more expressive. I was searching for God. I so wanted to believe that He loved me, but I had so much resentment in my heart towards Him that I was unable to trust Him and believe I could be included in His plan for mankind. I left the church and decided that I was just not comfortable there and could never be like the people that attended. I made other friends and soon started to drink and have my first experiences with worldly pleasures.

One of my new friends was several years older than me and into riding dirt bikes. He had a dirt bike and would frequently ride in the desert. I wanted to experience this, so I bought a beat-up bike, and he and I restored it. Of course, I had never ridden a dirt bike, so this was new for me. Shortly after my bike was restored, we were riding about five miles off the main road in the desert. What happened next forever changed me. I was leading, and he was riding behind me. We were riding around a sand dune, and I collided head on with another biker. I fell off my bike and landed on my back. His bike jumped my body like a ramp, driving my ribs into my left lung, which popped like a balloon. I blacked out. When I woke, my friend was holding me up so I would not fall asleep. If I had, I probably would have died. I was taken by ambulance to the base hospital, where they removed my spleen. I am forever left with a scar from the surgery. One thing that saved my life was the chest protector I was wearing. Even bigger than the chest protector, the Lord was looking out for me. When I was living in sin and wanted nothing to do with Him, He had His hand on me. It would be many years down the road before I could let my guard down long enough to let Him in.

I encourage you, if you are in a similar situation as I was at this time in my life, don't put off His invitation as I did. We are not promised tomorrow. Today is the day for you to receive Him. I mention this because it is true. Had I taken His promises to heart at this time in my life, He would have saved me, and I would have not experienced more troubles.

For He says: "In an acceptable time I have heard you, And in the day of salvation I have helped you." Behold, now is the acceptable time; behold, now is the day of salvation.

2 CORINTHIANS 6:2

I was stationed at Holloman Air Force Base for roughly two years. I exchanged the sands of the Southwest for a year in the Netherlands in Northern Europe. The Air Force called it a remote tour, but it was not remote in location, and I was able to expand my life experience immensely. One of the great benefits of being in Europe is you are close to everything. I made friends, and we learned how to utilize the vast rail system that our host country and continent had to offer. In the year I was stationed in Holland, I visited Belgium, England, Germany, and Austria and traveled all throughout my host country. The Netherlands offers extensive bike paths with enlarged sidewalks for bicycles and scooters. Most of these paths run parallel to most main and secondary roads. I never owned a bike, but the Dutch utilized the paths to the fullest.

You will never have outstanding french fries until you visit a street vendor in Holland. They are so bad for you, but so good. The preparation for these delicious, but not healthy, fries starts with dropping them in grease for several minutes, then removing them. The process is very similar to parboiling vegetables in water. When ordered, they put them back in the fryer and finish until fully cooked. They are full of grease, fat, and everything that is so good, but so bad, all wrapped into one. They top them off with fritessaus. I am still not sure what is in fritessaus, but it looks somewhat like mayonnaise. Regardless, Americans never questioned it; we loved it. I am so glad I was twenty years old when I was over there. My body would never be able to handle that many calories, grease, or fat at fifty-seven.

When I left the Netherlands, I was sent to Sicily for another one-year tour. The base in Sicily was more remote than the one I had just left, but I was able to function and get around to see the sights. The best part of this region is the food. Pizza is so much different in Sicily than in the United States. Over there, they put everything and anything onto a pie. It almost looks like they clear out the refrigerator and load up the pizza before putting it in the oven. I saw corn, octopus, and other oddities on pizza. I would never eat octopus, but it was a hit for the adventurous of us. I enrolled in college with the University of Maryland, European division, and took several classes, mainly in English and literature, before heading back to the United States. I had taken my first class at my last duty station. It was a video class on early American history with the City Colleges of Chicago.

These two years overseas were good for me on many levels. I was able to travel and see places and experience cultures most people my age had not. Enrolling in college and starting classes gave me purpose. Instead of drinking the years away like a lot of airmen did, I focused on my studies and travel. I could have very easily fallen into the trap of partying, but I wanted more, so I started my search towards fulfillment. I thought I was getting off to a good start, working towards goals that were responsible and productive. I had a hole in my heart that I was trying to fill with the things in this world, but I would never find true fulfillment until I gave my life to Jesus. The things and pleasures of this world will someday come to an end. Then where will any of us be if we put our trust and faith in this world? Of course, I did not know this at the time and thought if I worked harder, established more goals, and met the right person to complete me, I would arrive and be content in myself. I was so wrong on every level, but I kept pressing forward because it was the only thing

I knew to do. If you feel this way, I encourage you to keep on reading. I've been where you are and can relate to how you feel. I've been there, and the only thing I can say at this point is that God will do for all what He does for one.

For all that is in the world—the lust of the flesh,
the lust of the eyes, and the pride of life—
is not of the Father but is of the world.

1 JOHN 2:16

So far, in my short military career, I had already been stationed at three active Air Force bases. The Netherlands and Sicily were both one-year tours, and I was starting to feel very transient. My sister had moved to Florida and had recently gotten married. I was not able to attend her wedding since I was overseas, but I wanted to be relatively close to her, so I put in for Florida. I received orders to MacDill Air Force Base in Tampa. This was a whole new environment for me as I had never lived in a big city or close to the beach. I quickly learned to enjoy the amenities of a large city and the beauty and peace that the Florida beaches provided. I enrolled in Saint Leo University and attended classes the duration of my time in Florida. As I mentioned, I was searching for fulfillment and purpose. Soon, I started to drink and partake in more of what the world had to offer. Have you ever reached a point in your life where you just can't take any more? I was quickly heading in that direction. I had no stability in my life. Yes, I was attending college, had a career, had friends, and always had plenty to do during my off time, but I was empty and hollow and just could not figure out where I had gone wrong and why I felt the way I did. The bottom of my life fell out when a guy I had been dating dumped me. I had never been in love and was heartbroken. I had nowhere to turn and no one who would understand how I felt. Up to this point, nobody had ever loved me. I had a really hard time grasping that I was not good enough for him. What changed? How had this happened? Am I that bad of a person? I regressed and entered a deep depression that lasted for several weeks.

But God was about to show up in my life and work in me. I was desperate and had heard that God was there for any who would turn to Him, but I did not think that applied to me. In my opinion, His invitation was only for those who did not battle the demons that I had. I felt cornered and doomed to live out my life, however long or short it would be, carrying the burdens of my shame, guilt, and sin. At the time, I felt more rejected than anything. After all, if Chris rejected me, why should I expect anything less from Jesus? I am so glad I was wrong! There must have been a spark of hope tucked away deep in the recesses of my life because I started to recall memory verses I had learned as a child in Sunday school.

I started to watch *The 700 Club* in small doses. I felt drawn to this program while, at the same time, I believed I could never be like any of these perfect people on television. It was painful and difficult for me to face, but I decided to go forward in the only way I knew, with a few changes. For the moment, I was too hurt to trust anyone, especially a man. I enjoyed listening to Sheila Walsh on *The 700 Club*. I watched and listened to her and the other host pray for people while on the air. Many of their prayers were for people who were afflicted with sickness and disease. I was totally healthy, but on the inside, I was hollow, empty, and crying out for someone who could provide the answers to life I have been asking myself for a very long time. I decided to write a letter to Sheila Walsh with my story, and I could not help but ask why God was only interested in helping those who were physically sick. I really needed help. I was desperate but still drawn to watch their program. I never did get a direct response to my question, but I did notice after I wrote my concerns that they were also praying for people who fell closer to my category. God was starting to move in my life, and I did not even realize it. He was the one who kept my focus and sparked the glimmer of hope that I could someday have a fulfilled life in Him. He was slowly revealing His love for me, and I had no idea He was about to really show up strong and expel all of the lies of the enemy.

I yearned to know that God could reach, change, and save a homosexual. As I get further into my testimony, I never came to God to become a heterosexual. I later accepted Him because I was in dire need of a Savior. He was the one I had looked for; He was the one who created the empty space in my heart that only He could fill. What happened is that the Lord convicted me of my sin and my need for Him. That is what changed me. He is the expert at taking broken people and forming them into His masterpiece.

God met me where I was and made a way for me to get to Him. I was beyond left field; I was in a life preserver in the middle of the ocean alone. Thank God that He was the life preserver.

I came into contact with a man from a church in Orlando. He had been gay and now claimed to be a Christian. Oh boy! Normally, this would have gone over like a ton of bricks, but considering my state, I was open to seeing if this was real. I met him by calling the church, and someone patched me through to his office. This church had a ministry for homosexuals. I spoke with him several times, and he invited me to come to Orlando for a church service. It is funny; during this time, I felt everything inside me telling me to go and telling me it was fake and a ploy to either expose me or get money.

I had been raised in a church that did not treat homosexuals or anyone that did not fit their mold well. This was new to me. How could these people have compassion for me? After all, I had been exposed and molested by a Christian at a church camp. Curiosity, along with my need for fulfillment, got the best of me, and I decided to drive to Orlando. God started working on me long before this service and *The 700 Club*. He was setting me up for good things. Salvation was His plan for me, and I didn't see it coming. I arrived at the church, and the service was much different than I had experienced as a child. The people treated me very well. For the first time in my life, I felt welcomed at a church. During the service, God worked on my heart. I felt the presence of God and realized I had a deep need for Him. I believed that what I needed was Him and knew that if anyone could change me and give me a purpose, He would. I gave my life to Him and surrendered to Him that night. My heart and mind were filled with joy and peace for the first time ever. The man that invited me (Lou) and his coworker (Roxanne) took me into the back room after the service and prayed with me and gave me some vital instructions to assure I stayed on the path the Lord had just put me on. One of the things they discussed was my need to be a part of a church that would help me grow in my relationship with Jesus. This was all so new, and under the old way of thinking, it would have seemed like too much. I just knew in my heart that He would lead and guide me to where I needed to be.

I went home to Tampa and asked the Lord, "What now?" Beyond the recommendations to find a church and get plugged in, I did not know where to go or where to start. I still had no direction, but there was a peace that let me know that everything would be alright. I entered a support group through a church that ministered to men and women who were coming out of the gay lifestyle. These were people like me who had given their lives to God but needed support. This was right up my alley, and I benefited immensely. I also started to attend a church near the University of South Florida. This church was small and met in a strip mall. The people were genuine and loved the Lord. I grew and became a member, volunteered, and tithed. My surroundings on the outside seemed to change quicker than the change on the inside. Oh, I was saved and redeemed by God—that was a complete and done work. The process of changing old ways of thinking, acting, and dealing with everyday life will take a lifetime, but He had definitely started on me. I ran into some well-meaning Christians who thought that everything would be different for me overnight. Yes, I was saved and redeemed, but I still had so much to walk through.

Being confident of this very thing,
that He who has begun a good work in you
will complete it until the day of Jesus Christ.

PHILIPPIANS 1:6

One of the issues I had to deal with was what I would do when Chris tried to contact me. I knew he would, and he did. I will never forget the phone call I received from him one day. He told me he was concerned about me and wanted to see how I was. I told him I had received Jesus into my life and was a changed person. He said some choice words. I told him I would not be able to have any contact with him unless he gave his life to the Lord. That was the last time I had contact with him.

Shortly after this conversation, I was notified by the Air Force that I would be deploying to Desert Storm. The war had already started, and I was to be temporary relief on a ninety-day rotation. While in Riyadh, I got closer to God and was able to be sustained with the fellowship of other believers I had come into contact with. I was in Saudi Arabia that year for Thanksgiving and can honestly say it was one of the most memorable holidays I had experienced. The friends I had made (men and women) contributed to our Thanksgiving meal. We were all connected and helped each other make it through this time of separation from our families. Thankfully, I was able to be back in the United States for Christmas. My parents and uncle picked me up in Philadelphia, and I went back to Ohio for Christmas.

When I returned to Florida, I received orders to Osan AB, South Korea. I now had a new life in God and had been set free. All was going well. For the first time, I was looking forward to what life had to offer through God.

5

A Fresh Start

MY LIFE WAS STARTING TO TAKE SHAPE. I WAS START-ing to learn how to fit in a little with the new life God had gifted me. I received a promotion just prior to leaving Flor-ida. Things were looking up. I knew that wherever I landed, Jesus would have a plan and take care of me. I so wanted to be a part of the body of Christ and serve, learn, and fit in. The dynamics of my past were still a hurdle, even though the Lord had completely redeemed me from sin and death.

My tour at Osan AB was the same length as those in Holland and Sicily (one year). I soon met other Chris-tians and was involved in the base chapel programs. There was also a ministry in the local town outside of the base's main gate called "The Hospitality House." This was a wonderful place for military members to spend time with other believers in a social environment. The facility was run by a missionary named Brad and his wife. They were civilians assigned to the Hospitality House, as I was to the Air Force Base. Every week or so, we would gather for a homemade meal prepared by someone different. This would draw a crowd from the base. We would have a Bible study afterwards, followed by a time of prayer and sharing. This was so comforting and nice and a far cry from what I had been accustomed to. My life had changed from running with wild men to studying God's Word on a Saturday night with other people who shared my new-found belief in Jesus.

During this year, I continued my undergraduate education as a part-time student. Even though I was saved and a child of God, I still had issues and trauma from my past that God was already helping me resolve. One of the issues I struggled with was defensiveness. I learned to not only stand up for myself, but to challenge anyone who had issues. My background has also made me very sensitive to treating all with dignity.

There was an incident in one of my classes during my off-duty time. One of the instructors seemed to single out a young lady based on her race. This went on every day. One day, I had had enough and decided to file a formal complaint with the university. My complaint quickly reached the top. Since it happened on a military installation, I was called into the office and questioned. I stood by my complaint and told them that this young lady should have never been treated in this manner. This was not a good learning environment, and no one else in the class was willing to address this issue, so I did. I wanted to mention this because my whole life, I never fit in and always felt alienated. Since I have always felt like an outcast, I was able to have empathy for this young lady. God was already refining my approach to these types of sensitive situations, and I knew it. Jesus can and will use this part of my personality in a way that bears His fruit and brings Him glory. These feelings have taken some time to soften. Prior to my conversion, I was very brazen and full of bitterness and anger. Most, if not all, my anger was directed towards Christians. I did not know why, but the sexual abuse I had been through taught me that nobody else would take care of me, but me. This was so misguided, but it was all I knew at the time. The Lord had protected me because I could not find my way out of a paper bag. The Bible says that while I was yet a sinner, He died for me (Romans 5:8), and that is exactly what sustained me through all the years I lived in rebellion.

Jesus has done the same for you as well. He is no respecter of persons. What He does for one, He will do for all. None of us deserve His grace, but He freely gives it to us because it cost Him everything. That is why His gift is so precious (Psalm 103:10, 17).

The year I was stationed in Korea was a year of growth but also a time of trial and temptation. Everything was coming together, but at times, it felt like it was falling apart. I had been hospitalized with gastrointestinal issues. I was in the hospital for several days and on rest for several more. I made a full recovery and was soon back to myself.

Several times, I was tempted to partake in familiar pleasures I had laid at the foot of the cross. The reality of the need for human companionship is at the center of everyone. God created us to be with others, but in His proper context. I am a firm believer in intimacy within the confines of God's Word. Honestly, I became very lonely at times. If it was not for God's mercy and intervention, I'm not sure I would have stayed on the path. I was a new Christian, and even though there were people in my life who were also saved and loved Jesus, I could not open up about my struggles, temptations, and what I had come out of to come to Jesus. He definitely supernaturally sustained me, and I kept my focus on Him and what He had me doing. I learned to keep my eyes on Christ and trust Him. Keeping our eyes on Him and trusting Him is something we will all have to do regularly until we go home to be with Him. I love how the Scripture says:

If then you were raised with Christ, seek those things which are above, where Christ is, sitting at the right hand of God. Set your mind on things above, not on things on the earth. For you died, and your life is hidden with Christ in God.

COLOSSIANS 3:1-3

At this time, I was redeemed, saved, and filled with the Holy Spirit. I also loved Jesus and believed everything I read in the Bible. However, I had not yet dealt with the trauma I had experienced years ago at summer camp. I did not know what I was going to do with the dynamics of my past and how to continue on the path set before me.

One thing that was comforting was reading the Bible. I found that many of the people the Lord put in places of influence and used mightily were really a mess. David was an adulterer and murderer (2 Samuel 11), and God called him a man after God's own heart (1 Samuel 13:14, Acts 13:22). Jonah ran from God after given clear direction (Jonah 1:3), but he came to himself, repented, and the Lord used him. Peter denied Christ three times (Matthew

26:69-75) and later went on to evangelize and be used by the Holy Spirit.

I identify mostly with Paul. He did not like Christians, and to call his treatment of Christians anything less than barbaric would be an understatement. Of course, I do not believe in this treatment, but I did not like Christians as Paul had prior to his conversion. He did everything he could to stop what Jesus had started. It is very interesting that in Paul's case and mine, that while we were fighting the truth, we got absorbed into the body of Christ. Paul's Damascus Road experience forever changed him (Acts 9). Paul went on to take the world by storm for the gospel. In his time, many came to know Jesus, and he wrote almost half of the New Testament by the direction of the Holy Spirit.

These are just a few accounts of people in the Bible who were not perfect and had very rough pasts. Reading these gave (and still does) me hope that God could not only keep me, but also use me. When I felt like giving up, I took comfort in the fact that Jesus did not expect me to be perfect, but He does expect me to be pliable in His hands. We are no different today than these people I have just mentioned. God met them where they were and used them because He knew their heart amidst all the confusion, sin, and turmoil they had going on. Jesus does not see you the way that you or others see you. He died so all could have a chance. He sees what you can become in Him, not what you are currently outside of Him. He is the center and will always be in that place.

The Lord is not slack concerning His promise, as some count slackness, but is longsuffering toward us, not willing that any should perish but that all should come to repentance.

2 PETER 3:9

My time in Korea was ending, and I received orders to Hawaii. Wow, I did not see that coming. Out of all the places I could be stationed, I never thought it would be Hawaii. When I left Korea, I was able to return to the United States and have my car shipped to Oahu. I had left it at my parent's house in Ohio while I was in Korea and missed it so. Both myself and my car arrived safely in Hawaii. My new start had literally taken me around the world from Florida to Korea to Honolulu.

If you've ever been to Hawaii, you know there is not a better place on the planet for warm summers and winters alike. I was able to see so much and create many memories. The Air Force base was located right next to Pearl Harbor, and I spent quite a bit of time there. The military presence is quite heavy on Oahu, with a Marine base on the other side of the island. All branches are relatively close in a very small amount of space. I continued in my higher education with Wayland Baptist University, Hawaii campus, and graduated in 1994 with a bachelor's in business administration, with a minor in behavioral science.

My job with the Air Force required extensive travel throughout the Pacific area. I have been back to Korea twice, Okinawa, Guam, and Alaska, all on temporary duty. I will say Alaska is definitely one of the most picturesque places on the planet. The beauty there is magnificent. It is sort of ironic. I was stationed in Hawaii and was able to travel to Alaska, two places with great beauty but different in climate and topography. I enjoyed this part of my job and really liked the travel. When I was not traveling, I was able to enjoy a normal daily routine.

I started attending a very large church in Honolulu. This was my first experience with a mega church, and I really enjoyed the people. I served in the tape room. This was in the days when the messages were recorded on cassette tapes and provided for those who wished to have a copy of the message immediately after the service. I joined what they called a life group that met once a week. We would gather and read the Bible, pray, and encourage each other in our walk with Jesus. I made plenty of friends and developed close friendships with several people. One of my friends and his wife were from Washington State. They had moved to Hawaii and lived in Waikiki. I loved going to their apartment to meet and fellowship. We regularly broke bread and just spent quality time together. There were several others who would meet with us. I had developed a circle of friends, and for the first time in my life, I felt accepted. It was an awkward feeling, but I enjoyed it and recognized that the Lord was changing me. I had been through so much change in such a short amount of time since I received Jesus. I had been to the Gulf War and had many changes that were all a part of God's plan for my life.

With all of this going on, I started to feel homesick and knew my time in Hawaii would be ending. I had seen so much and grown in the Lord, but I just had the desire to return to Ohio. I had been attending the Bible college at our church and decided to apply for an early separation from the Air Force and apply for Bible college in Columbus, Ohio. Columbus was quite the distance from Youngstown, but I knew this would be the next step in my journey. My application for early separation was approved. I was on my way to Ohio. At this time, the Gulf War was winding down, and the services were looking to downsize. Had it been any other time, I would not have been able to do this. The church I attended gave me their blessing and prayed for me. I arrived in Columbus in September 1996 and started Bible college the following spring.

Becoming a civilian was another change I had to adapt to. This was not an easy adjustment, but with God's help and guidance, I made the adjustment well. I started to attend the church that would be my host for Bible college. The church was very large, and I almost felt lost with all the people. I had to work and have insurance, so I got a job with UPS, loading and unloading trailers. The work was hard, but I made it.

This part of my account is probably one of the most difficult to write. In Columbus, I attended the church and Bible college regularly. I tithed and volunteered when my schedule between work and school permitted. After a year, I felt run down and hopeless. I had been through so much change, and God had always been there, but now, I felt like God had abandoned me. I was unable to connect with anyone in Columbus like I had in Hawaii and had very little to no social life. The world and familiar false senses of comfort brought on by the enemy were battering down my door. I did not know what to do. I felt all alone. How could God do this to me? I sounded like the children of Israel when they complained about how their life as slaves in Egypt was better than being free and heading for the Promised Land. I was not ready to think this logically. All I knew was that I felt alone and had nobody to call on. I never wanted to believe that God was not for me. I never wanted to believe that His Word was not true and His promises were unsound. I never wanted to believe that my only option was to run to my past. In my heart, I did not want to be a part of what the world had to offer. Up to this point, I had served the Lord for six years, but my faith was shipwrecked. I walked away from God. This was the biggest mistake of my life. I stepped out of His protection and did not know if I would be back. My life was taking a dangerous turn, and I chose to go down that road. A road that kept me out of fellowship with my Lord for twenty-three years.

I encourage you if you are at a place in your life where you have had it and you think God has abandoned you, don't give up on Him. I was wrong! He will always be there for you when you call on Him and will meet you where you are at. I paid a very heavy price for my decision, and I do not recommend it to anyone.

For "whoever calls on the name
of the Lord shall be saved."

ROMANS 10:13

Let your conduct be without covetousness; be content with
such things as you have. For He Himself has said, "I will
never leave you nor forsake you."

HEBREWS 13:5

Had I known this Scripture and taken it to heart, I may
have not given up and given in.

6

I Ran

I DID NOT HAVE A PLAN FOR WHAT WOULD HAPPEN next. Since I knew "everything," I was going to pave my own way and be my own boss. I was determined not to let myself down as I thought God had. You know, the hard thing for someone who has been touched by God and redeemed is that I was marked by God, and He was not going to let me go without a pursuit. Just as the children of Israel wandered in the desert for forty years, so did I for twenty-three. I will say before I go any further that this is not the way to go if you are contemplating it! God never left me, but at the time, I was in rebellion against Him and His plan for my life.

I left the church and lost all contact with the few Christian acquaintances I had made. I fell off the face of the church's radar and sunk into the depths of sin, despair, and, later, regret. I was running with the party crowd and soon found that I enjoyed the pleasures of sin and companionship. It took some time, but I established friendships with people who shared my old views prior to my conversion. Of course, I never spoke about the Lord to them because my focus was now on me, not Him.

Our group had a regular routine, which usually involved a lot of drinking and late-night carousing. Late nights usually involved coming home still drunk at five the next morning. I was running with wild men and did not care. The Bible does say sin is pleasurable, but a passing pleasure (Hebrews 11:24-26), and I was enjoying all of it. I had excuses for everything I was doing. I now had friends. The people at church never befriended me, but these new people were more than willing to spend time with me.

The problem with these lies is that Satan can only copy an original that God created. He cannot create, only plagiarize. I had made acquaintances, not friends, and there is a difference. If I had waited on God, I would have been blessed with real friends, not mere people to fill a square. While I write my account, I am trying to point out what I did and how I now realize I bought into a lie. I had turned my back on the only person who was ever there for me. His name is Jesus, and I was already starting to miss Him, but did not know if I would ever be able to go back (another lie). His promise to never leave me in Hebrews 13:5 and Joshua 1:9 dispels this lie.

Since I was tired and growing weary of drinking and not having any formidable relationships, I decided it was time for me to think about settling down and having a true relationship with a man. One that went beyond drinking and one-night stands. I needed to have stability in my life, and I got what I so wanted.

I would like to add my take on what I was going through emotionally at this time. One reason gays and lesbians are very defensive, especially towards Christians, is that often people do not come across as genuine and caring. They seem to only want to prove that they are right. People can see right through that, and it gets us nowhere. There is another reason for the heightened defensive posture. Speaking from my own experience, it took me a long time to accept my same-sex attractions. By a long time, I mean a lifetime. The sexual abuse clouded my heart and gave me a hard start on how I not only saw God, but men as well. Eventually, I accepted that was how I was supposed to be and vowed to never let anyone take that from me. This was one reason I could not stand to deal with Christians. I want to mention this because I encourage my brothers and sisters in Christ not to try to win an argument with anyone. Live like Jesus and show them His love. I am not saying not to witness and share the gospel—by all means that is what we are called to do—just be sensitive. My challenge is for you to see the person as Jesus does. You have so much, my brothers and sisters, to offer a hurting world that so needs the One you have already met. But back to my story.

If you were online back in 2001, you would remember instant messaging on AOL. I was one of those who had an account. Someone I knew in New York introduced me to someone in Cleveland. His name was Joe, and we started instant messaging each other. We realized we might have a connection and started to talk on the phone. The more we spoke on the phone, the more we wanted to meet. This was difficult since he lived in Cleveland, and I was in Columbus. It took three months, but we agreed to meet in Cleveland for the weekend. I felt good about this. Everything I had been looking for was finally coming to pass. I would finally have a relationship with meaning and purpose. One that was not centered around sex or what he or I could get out of the other.

Our first meeting, and the day we considered our anniversary, was October 10, 2001. This was a very hard time for our country, with 9/11 happening about a month prior. I remember Joe got a speeding ticket on 9/11/2001. This was ironic since he was a police officer in a neighboring municipality. He was a very kind man, unlike many I had come to know. My life was starting to take shape. For the first time, I had friends, a new condo, a job, and now, the start of a promising relationship. I was complete; I had found someone who seemed to care about me. Everything looked good.

Over the next three years, we got to know each other and established, not only a relationship, but a friendship as well. We became best friends but were still living over one hundred miles apart. My time in the church and with the Lord seemed like a distant memory. During my entire relationship with Joe, I never spoke of the Lord until the end.

Living outside of God's protection and plan does not come without consequences. I was diagnosed with Hepatitis B around this time. I never got sick but was a carrier. I was completely upfront with Joe when we met about this. His reaction was one of acceptance, love, and compassion. Additionally, since I had no manifested symptoms of Hepatitis and was otherwise healthy, he dismissed my diagnosis as incorrect. Originally, my doctor was considering a treatment that involved many shots. They told me that this treatment would make me sick and to get immediate help if I had any thoughts of suicide. Since Joe and I still lived apart from each other, and I lived alone, I decided to adopt a dog to keep me busy and active. I ended up adopting a white German Shepherd named Shyloh. This was not a good decision, but I did it anyhow. My physician changed his mind about my treatment and referred me to a doctor much closer to my house. My new doctor treated me with medication, and I was under their thumb until the virus passed through my body well into 2006. It never made me sick, and to this day, I have no side effects from the disease, but I did have a new four-legged friend who desperately needed me.

Shyloh had been abused. He was grossly underweight and did not trust anyone. He immediately took to me, and I learned how to love, care, and give myself to a living creature who needed a second chance. To this day, it breaks my heart to write this account because I can still see him in need. I had saved him from the hands of the man who treated him with cruelty. This would never happen under my care. I was determined to care for him. Joe had a dog named Lucy. She was a beagle/dachshund mix. Her story was very similar to Shyloh's. Joe was still on the police force when we met, and he rescued her during an animal abuse call. The people he rescued her from abused her beyond my ability to comprehend. How can people treat animals this way? I could, and still do, not understand why someone would be so cruel. Dogs are very special, and I believe God made them to show the greatest amount of love that any animal is capable of to people.

When Shyloh and Lucy met, they were immediately best friends. She was small and introverted because of the abuse, and he was much larger and stronger. I remember they would play tug for hours. They both came out of their shells and formed a very special bond with each other. Their companionship brought them both much healing. They were broken, but they were being restored just by having each other. I could go on for hours about these two dogs.

Having them also drew Joe and I closer, and our relationship grew stronger. The difference between the dogs and us was that they could experience healing with each other's companionship. However, we needed the hand of God to touch us and make us whole. Of course, we did not see this and would have refused to believe that was truly what we needed.

God has made a special place in each of us for Him. No other person can occupy this space but God. When we try to place someone else in this spot, we end up unfulfilled and unhappy with our lives. This is God's spot because we are His creation. Even though Joe and I could never complete each other, our lives were as broken as our dogs' past. We were happy on the outside, but hollow, hurting, and empty on the inside.

We decided that our three-year long-distance relationship was getting old, and we both wanted to be together. In January 2004, Joe relocated to Columbus with his company. I had just started working for the Postal Service as a mailman. We were now together under one roof.

For the next fifteen years, we lived together and shared our lives. Joe and I had completely different childhoods, and at times, that made for a challenge. He was raised in a house with an alcoholic father. His childhood had been very difficult. He learned how to cope with the arrows from his early childhood and was able to do well and make sound decisions. I, on the other hand, had been raised in the church but did not accept Him as Lord and Savior until much later in life. The bottom line is that on the outside, our lives were together, but on the inside, we were missing the only one who could satisfy. We needed Jesus desperately.

I can honestly say that there was not a day that went by that I didn't think about the Lord. I longed to go back, but I felt stuck and trapped. I believed the lie that I had been too bad. The enemy was right there, telling me that God would never want me back. I had a real encounter with God; I had known Him. I walked away and wanted to return to my Jesus in the worst way. I would often talk to Him and tell Him I wanted to return, but I had no way. I was terrified. Of course, I never spoke to Joe about Jesus and God's plan for salvation. I was hollow, empty, and desperate.

In 2014, we traveled to Maryland and were legally married. Two years later, I decided to legally change my last name to his. I wanted to be close to him and feel like a married couple. My family did not support me and even said I could no longer be their son if I changed my name. This hurt immensely. They were more upset about me changing my last name than about the sexual abuse I had endured as a child. This caused a rift between my parents and myself for quite some time. The good news is there was restoration, but it took a while.

In 2017, I transferred from a carrier to a clerk in the Postal Service. This was a job I had applied for a year prior. I had a supervisor named Gail, who was a Christian. She was the first Christian since I fell away that treated me with respect and courtesy. She told me about Jesus and shared about her past and how she came to the Lord. I remember that after a while, I started to get a glimmer of hope that maybe I was not too far gone, maybe Jesus did still love me, maybe I was not damaged beyond repair. Gail was the kindest person I have ever met, and God used her to impact me. Of course, at the time, I did not realize that, but I hoped this was the case. I watched her very closely to see if she would swear or give me any reason to discredit her commitment to the Lord. Of course, nobody is perfect, but Gail never wavered. She always lived like Jesus for everyone in our office.

Things on the outside were still looking good, even though I felt like a dead man walking on the inside. This was soon about to change because Joe and I were about to enter the fight of our lives.

7

God's Mercy

I STRUGGLED WITH A NAME FOR THIS CHAPTER, not because it is not appropriate, but because God's mercy is always right on. This is a heavy-duty part of my story. Even in the midst of what you are about to read, God's mercy triumphed over judgement. God was about to pour out His abundant mercy on both of us during the most difficult circumstances we had to deal with.

But God, who is rich in mercy, because of His great love
with which He loved us, even when we were
dead in trespasses, made us alive together with Christ
(by grace you have been saved).

EPHESIANS 2:4-5

Around Thanksgiving 2018, Joe started to have health issues. Whenever he ate, he would throw up. He could not keep anything down. At the very beginning, neither of us thought much about it, figuring it would pass. Unfortunately, it got worse, and he started to lose weight quickly. I told him he needed to see our family doctor immediately, but he would not! Instead, he promised to go in after the holidays. In January 2019, our doctor sent Joe in for an endoscopy. The results of the procedure confirmed the worst possible outcome. Joe was diagnosed with esophageal cancer.

Since he had waited several months to go in, and it is a very fast-moving cancer, we were behind the power ball with treatment. I was not expecting this. I figured he had an ulcer in his stomach or some other issue. Cancer never crossed my mind. When the doctor gave us the news, Joe was still coming out of anesthesia. I passed out, and they had to revive me. Since I am a diabetic, the staff was concerned about my blood sugar. I came around, and I will never forget what one of the nurses told me. She said, "He needs you now more than ever." I responded, "He has me. He is my husband, and I took vows to him." From that moment, I decided no matter what it took, I was going to be there for him. And that is what I did over the next year.

Since Joe was not coherent when the doctor gave us the news, I was the one to break it to him. This was very difficult, but I had no choice. How do you tell your spouse and best friend they have cancer? What's the plan? How will we manage? What will I do if and when I lose him? I had not yet given my life back to the Lord, and the hope that I had built my life on had just been removed. I was scared. This news crippled us emotionally. We were not sure how to process it. All of our dreams had just been taken from us; our plans dashed on the rocks of life. Fortunately, there was one rock we would later cling to. He was the only answer. We were unaware of this at this time, but He soon showed up in a way I never expected.

I applied for FMLA and was able to make every one of Joe's appointments—labs, chemotherapy, surgery, radiation, office visits, and later, immunotherapy. We were both heartbroken and felt lost. We had dreams of moving to the Dayton, Ohio, area after I retired. We had already picked out the area we liked. That had become our biggest goal. Now, this happened, and we were stranded. Our hearts were broken. Everything had changed after just one visit to the doctor. Joe and I had no support structure in place with friends and family. I felt the weight of it all. I tried to protect him while caring for him, our dogs, and myself.

On January 23, 2019, Joe had his first of many PET scans at Riverside Methodist Hospital in Columbus. While we were in the waiting room, the most amazing thing happened. Joe was unaware of what I was experiencing, but God had started to chip away at my stony, bitter, and lost soul. I will never forget this day for the rest of my life. He was about to change me forever. As we were waiting, there was an elderly couple who were there with their son-in-law. They were talking about Jesus while waiting for their appointment. The wife had been diagnosed with stomach cancer, and their son-in-law was there for support. I remember this elderly, sweet couple had so much peace in the darkest moment of their lives, unlike what Joe and I were experiencing in similar circumstances. The elderly man spoke loudly enough for me to hear their entire story and many aspects of their faith in the Lord. I was meant to hear this. I hope the day will come when I can meet these dear people in heaven. Their faith and love for Jesus and each other spoke to my deepest needs.

After listening to them talk, I remember thinking I so wanted the peace that they had and the joy that they emulated, even in the worst of circumstances. I had no answers. My house of cards had crumbled with this diagnosis. Everything I held dear was being taken from me. Joe was all I had. He was my spouse and best (only) friend. The staff finally called Joe back for his appointment, and I headed over to the main hospital via the underground tunnel connecting the cancer center to the main facility. I grabbed a bite to eat and felt numb. How was I supposed to cope? What would I do if and when Joe died? How would I care for our two dogs alone? How was I supposed to make it through his treatment, be there for him, and continue to work? This was all so overwhelming.

On my way back to the cancer center, I took the same route through the tunnel. As I was walking, I decided to stop and sit down. The hospital had benches and seating in the tunnel, and I took advantage of this to clear my thoughts. As I sat, I got this strong feeling that I needed to reach out to God. How could I do that, though? I had walked away. I was lost. I was damaged goods. Something had to change, and soon, because I was desperate. The earlier encounter I had in the waiting room with the elderly couple flooded my mind. I so wanted Jesus. I called a prayer line and remember thinking, I must be crazy.

There is a way that seems right to a man,
But its end is the way of death.

PROVERBS 14:12

The only prayer line I knew of was *The 700 Club*. I called and soon got to speak with a person who prayed for me and shared the Gospel of Jesus Christ. It was like I had never heard the message before. For the first time in years, I felt hope rising inside me. When I got off the phone, I was shaking and had to sit down. I started to speak with God and tell Him how much of a mess I had become and how I needed Him. I told Him that He could have my life and all of its troubles. I was sorry and asked for forgiveness for bailing on Him years ago. I told Him that if He could redeem my life, He could have what was left of it. I needed Him and asked Him to come into my life and change me forever. I did not know what else to do except be honest with Him. I expressed my need for Him and told Him that all of my manmade plans, dreams, and goals had crashed. Thank you, Lord, for redeeming my life!

Immediately, it was as if a well was springing up inside of me, giving me hope and encouraging me to trust Him. I had no church, knew no Christians, and the few friends Joe and I had had bailed after his diagnosis. I believed that God would sustain, protect, comfort, and guide me through my life, especially this time. I also had this immediate desire to pray for Joe. I decided right then and there to pray for him—to stand in the gap in prayer and faith to the Lord. I knew Joe would probably not live physically, but I was more concerned about where he would spend eternity. I had to pray for him. I had to believe that God would do a miracle in his life as He had just done in mine. I asked the Lord not to let death take him until he had the opportunity to either accept or reject Jesus as his Lord.

I emerged out of that tunnel a new man. I was redeemed. I now had the same hope that the elderly couple had. I sat and had a cup of coffee and let the day's events sink in. God had shown up and saved me, and I had a sense that everything would be alright. Jesus has a way of making everything right and giving us peace to make it even when the situations and circumstances have not yet budged. He has and is moving. My life on the outside was still a mess. Joe was still sick, and I had no friends and no idea how I would juggle taking off work for his care. All of this seemed so big, so I took it to the One who could handle it because I surely could not. If I learned anything from my backslidden state, it was that I could not be my own CEO; only Jesus could. He was the only one I wanted in that position. I had a sense of peace that He would handle all of my concerns, and I knew that everything, even Joe's salvation, would be alright. I was now in the hands of Almighty God, and I was lifting up Joe to the Lord.

I wish I could say the next year was easy. It was far from that, but it was possible because the Lord gave me the strength to make it. Without a support system in place, Joe's care, keeping the house going, and working all fell on me.

When I returned to the waiting room, Joe was finished with his appointment, and we headed home. I did not tell him what had happened to me in the tunnel because I felt led to let him see the undeniable changes in my life. I knew giving my life to Jesus would be a hard sell to him, and now was not the time to talk about it, but it was the time to see the buds of the fruit of the Spirit that were forming.

Joe's treatment was scheduled to begin soon. That same month, our furnace decided to quit working. January in Ohio without heat is not good. Joe was sick, and I had to get something figured out. I thank God for my parents, who really helped us out and were able to provide us with a new furnace. The company that installed the furnace was having a special at the time. Since we purchased a new furnace, we got a new A/C unit for free. This was too good to be true, but God was showing up strong and using situations to take care of both of us.

My application for FMLA was approved, and all the support facets to care for him were now in place, thanks to God. I was also fortunate that over the years, I had saved my sick leave, which I now needed. I told Gail that I had given my life to the Lord. She was so happy for me and knew God was going to make everything right. I was able to temporarily change my days off to accommodate Joe's chemotherapy and radiation treatments, which were on Mondays and lasted for six weeks.

I had been praying for Joe and was hoping for an opportunity to share the gospel with him. He did notice that my behavior was changing. I was no longer cussing and had more patience. He also saw me reading my Bible and praying. I'm sure he thought I was in a phase and would soon snap out of it and be back to my old self in no time. The truth is, my old self was no longer. I had been changed into a new creation by Jesus. Little did he know, I was praying for God to do the same thing for him.

I will never forget one evening Joe had gone to bed, and I was up watching television. I came upon a movie called *I Can Only Imagine*. The true story about how the group MercyMe was formed and the life of the lead singer for the group. This movie had me in tears because I could see the pain and hurt in the lives of Bart and his father. I also saw how God restored Bart and saved his father. This movie gave me hope that our situation and Joe hearing the gospel and receiving it were more real than ever. I had been reading the Bible and memorizing Scripture. My two favorite verses were in Proverbs and Philippians. I hung onto these promises (and still do). They have gotten me through a lot.

> *Trust in the LORD with all your heart,*
> *And lean not on your own understanding;*
> *In all your ways acknowledge Him,*
> *And He shall direct your paths.*
> *Do not be wise in your own eyes;*
> *Fear the LORD and depart from evil.*

PROVERBS 3:5-7

*Be anxious for nothing, but in everything by prayer
and supplication, with thanksgiving, let your requests be
made known to God; and the peace of God,
which surpasses all understanding, will guard your hearts
and minds through Christ Jesus.*

PHILIPPIANS 4:6-7

I read these verses repeatedly. What made their message so real was I could not understand in my own mind why all of this was happening. Trusting in Him was my only successful option so that is what I did. I could not be wise in my own judgements, nor could I explain this. I had no control, and for the first time, I was glad I did not. Additionally, I had no anxiety, only an inner peace that gave me complete assurance. My prayers started to change. I asked the Lord many times not to let death take Joe until he had an opportunity to accept or reject Him. I knew I was praying correctly because it is His will that none perish.

*The Lord is not slack concerning His promise,
as some count slackness, but is longsuffering toward us,
not willing that any should perish
but that all should come to repentance.*

2 PETER 3:9

I remember one day in April when I had to take Joe to the emergency room. He was admitted for observation, and I stayed by his side. It had just been three months since his diagnosis, and he was beginning to come to terms with the fact that he would not live. I cannot explain what it is like to see a loved one come to terms with their humanity by staring down death, but I can say it will change you forever. Throughout the next year, it did change me. I have come to grips with my own humanity through this. He was very angry with me for insisting he go to the hospital. I was concerned that he might die if we did not go. One of the biggest challenges for me was that I had to absorb all of it and fight every battle. When he had a bad day, he always took it out on me. I really think I never would have made it without Christ in my life. He was and is my strength. Joe later told me that he was concerned that he might never go home. I told him that I was out of answers for any of this, but said, "Jesus loves you more than I ever could, and He loves me more than you ever could." Jesus was my only answer. There was no other option. Jesus is the way, truth, and life, and I knew my Redeemer was alive and well and actively involved in all of this. I knew my marriage with Joe was not of the greatest importance. The most important issue of the day was his salvation. My eternal destiny was secure, but his was not yet.

Jesus said to him, "I am the way, the truth, and the life. No one comes to the Father except through Me."

JOHN 14:6

Shortly after he was released from the hospital, we received the results of the latest scans. Since both PET and CT scans showed no signs of cancer, we were sent to see a surgical oncologist to have the tumor removed. The visit went well, and Joe was scheduled for an exploratory surgery prior to the big one, where they would check to see if he was, in fact, cancer free. We were up at the hospital early, and I waited and prayed in the waiting room for the results. The surgeon brought the worst possible news. The cancer had moved to Joe's liver and ribs. He also told me that if they did the big surgery, the cancer would spread that much faster with exposure to oxygen. I did not know what to do except go to the Lord. My faith was now in Jesus, and I knew He had a plan to see us through. The surgeon sent us back to the oncologist, where Joe started immunotherapy. This was a newer treatment and had fewer side effects. Joe proved to be quite responsive to this treatment, which lasted from September to December 2019.

The Lord was with us, and I knew the prayers I was praying for Joe's salvation were reaching heaven. It is amazing how God showed up during this year of treatment. Every time I turned around, there was a Christian, who was empathetic and loving. God put His people in our paths to help us maneuver through what appeared to be impossible in our current situation. I was so grateful God had placed His people in our path. He was moving His mighty hand in our lives, and the peace He gave was sustaining as well as protecting us. For example, I received a call from our health insurance company. The woman who called me had spoken with me earlier and was a Christian. She called just to ask me how I was doing. There were no issues with claims. She was just moved by the Holy Spirit to call and check up on me. I had no Christian friends and was not attending church.

All of my time and energy was spent keeping Joe going. There was no time for me at all. I had to work and keep the house going. This was the toughest year of my life, but God was making a path and a way for me. I knew it, and Joe was starting to get it as well. He would see me reading my Bible. I witnessed to him and told him that Jesus loves him, and God is there for him, but he must ask Him to come into his life. He listened, and we watched *I Can Only Imagine* together. All I wanted out of this was for him to accept Jesus. I knew God was able, willing, and ready to give Joe a new start.

I saw not only Joe come to grips with his humanity, but I also saw him come to grips with his need for a Savior. One day in particular, during radiation, shortly after his diagnosis, it was very cold outside, and since he was the first patient of the day, the building was also chilly. He went back for his appointment, and there were some minor difficulties with the equipment. Joe told me he was so cold and was lying on the table with his hands above his head. In tears, he told me he told God he was so cold and asked Jesus to come into his life. At that time, he said he felt this warmth from the top of his head run down to his toes. Jesus had come into his life! He was now a new creation. I was so happy and grateful. Satan no longer had a claim on his life; he belonged to God. I saw God's peace rest on him and knew that all would be well.

Even though he had rough days, the peace of God rested on him until he took his final breath. I knew his time would be short, but it was difficult for me to process. I had known him for twenty years, and our lives were intertwined as friends and as a couple. Now, things had changed. Even though this was tough, to say the least, with eternity in mind, we were both in a much better place than we had been prior. Being sick and belonging to God is much better than being physically healthy with the devil. We were both spiritually healthy because of God's Spirit and redemption. It was unique in a sense. On one hand, I felt my life was falling apart, and on the other, I saw it being recreated. I thank God for His sovereign work in our lives. My biggest prayer had been answered. Joe was now a child of God!

This year bought other problems to our family. Joe's sister lost her husband unexpectedly to an aneurysm, and my sister went through a very messy divorce after a thirty-year marriage. Additionally, one of Joe's old friends was found dead in her home. It seemed like 2019 was the year of loss for our family. With all of this going on, Joe and I were safe, our destinations secure in Christ.

I cannot imagine how things could get tougher, but they soon did. Just before Christmas 2019, Joe started to have symptoms of a cold. At first, we did not think much of it because he was going through immunotherapy, and other than this, he was fine. He was due for his next set of scans, so we went in. When we did a follow-up with the doctor, he told us the cancer had come back with a vengeance, and the only thing we could do was maybe another form of chemo. Joe agreed to this for my benefit, but I told him he would have to make this decision for his own sake. I would be alright. He declined treatment, and we contacted hospice.

On the way home from the doctor's office, I told him again, "Jesus loves you more than I ever could." This conversation was around January 7.

Hospice visited our home on January 9. He was able to stay at home, and I stayed with him twenty-four hours a day. The hospice staff were outstanding and helped us in every way imaginable. The next day (January 10), I had a doctor's appointment. I told Joe I could stay home, but he insisted I go. When I returned home, he was at the kitchen table. He was not able to walk and needed help to go to the bathroom. This was the first time he had needed my help in the bathroom. He was very independent, and I never tried to take that away from him. He was also quickly losing his ability to speak. We sat on the couch. I told him that I loved him and that he was in God's hands. I also told him that it was alright for him to go. I would be okay. This was around 5:00 p.m.

After this, he started to throw up bile. I would wash out a rinse pan only to get it clean in time for him to use it again. Joe attempted to sleep on the couch, but I did not sleep. This eventually subsided, and he seemed to settle on the couch. I sat in my chair close by. This was around 8:30 p.m. As I sat in my chair, I began to sing "It Is Well with My Soul" and kept repeating the name of Jesus. I am not sure why I did, but I could not stop myself. This amazing peace came over me, and the whole home was enveloped in His presence. Joe had started to move like someone who could not get comfortable. The peace and presence got stronger, and I felt lost in the arms of God. Joe stopped moving, and at first, I thought, "Good, he fell asleep." He did; he had gone home to be with the Lord. The Holy Spirit's presence was so strong I could tell you without seeing where God's servants came into the house to take Joe home. I got up and turned on the lights. His eyes were open. He was gone. This all happened so fast, but I am glad I was there to care for him. I do not want to sound over spiritual, but this is what happened, and the peace I experienced was truly supernatural.

I am one of those people who do not like funerals or dead bodies. I do everything to avoid caskets. Since Joe died under the hospice umbrella, I should have called the hospice nurse. But I did not know this, so called 911 instead. The paramedics and police showed up first, and I explained what had happened. They declared him deceased on January 10, 2020, at 8:51 p.m. The hospice nurse still had to respond and so did the funeral home. My call to the wrong support agency delayed everything. Joe was deceased on the couch for over three hours before he could be taken to the funeral home. During this time, I had complete peace and knew God was with me. His presence was still so strong in the house, but not like it was when Joe passed. I am sure God had His angels around me, and I am so glad He did. What do you do when this situation happens? I did all I knew, and that was to believe my Lord. My battle was not over. This chapter was over, but I still had plenty to go through. Fortunately, I was not alone, and never would be again!

"Therefore do not worry about tomorrow, for tomorrow will worry about its own things. Sufficient for the day is its own trouble."

MATTHEW 6:34

8

All Things are New

THE SUNDAY BEFORE JOE'S PASSING, I ATTENDED church. The church bulletin mentioned a Christian group that was starting to help people work through the loss of a loved one. I so wanted to get closer to the Lord. I was hurting and not sure who to turn to, but I knew *whom* to turn to. Jesus had helped me through so much, and now that Joe was with Him, I knew I needed to get to a place where I could not only grow but also heal. I was totally exhausted from all the energy I had put into taking care of him, that I was left empty and hollow. If it had not been for Jesus, I would have really been in bad shape. God's Spirit sustained me. I was able to attend the grief support group, and it did wonders. I also started to attend church. I had no answers except that this was what I needed to do. My troubles and loss were not quite over. I still had to face two difficult decisions.

We had two dogs—Ethel and Alice. Since Joe was retired, they always had constant care. However, my life had just changed with his passing. I was now faced with the big question, "What do I do with them?" I was off work for a month but returned after the funeral. When I returned to work, I was unable to work an entire full day or week. I started slowly, and within a month or two, I was back to working a forty-hour week. My faith in the Lord Jesus and believing He had me was what I held onto. I soon realized that Alice had separation anxiety. Even with Ethel's companionship while I was at work, it was not enough for her. After much prayer, and pain, I called the shelter I had adopted her from. I explained my situation to them, and they were very empathetic. I told them I was not going to drop Alice off, but I wanted to foster her and be a part of the selection process for her new home. I am so grateful to the Lord. He provided the perfect home for her almost immediately. A young married couple was interested in her. They had a four-year-old female beagle, and Alice was a four-year-old coonhound. It was literally a match made in heaven. They loved her, and I was at complete peace about them adopting her.

Now it was just Ethel and myself. One evening, I came home from work and noticed something was wrong with Ethel. She could not stand. I was afraid I would lose her. This was in the early part of Covid, and I was not permitted to go into the vet with her. At her appointment, they came out and took her in the practice while I waited in my car. She was diagnosed with aspiration pneumonia. After I listened to the doctor's prognosis, I knew the most humane approach to this was to put her to sleep. She had helped me through so much with losing Joe. But now I was about to lose the last member of our family. In May 2020, I had her put to sleep. The house seemed very lonely with just me in it. These are the situations where God's presence shows up and He comforts, protects, and gives us enough to make it one more day. There were days I did not think I would make it. This was so much, but I had peace and Jesus, and that was what saw me through. Even though it looked like I was alone, I knew I was not.

I continued to seek after God for peace, understanding, and direction. I knew I had to get out of the house if I ever wanted a chance at a new life. I had twenty years of memories in the house and wanted to be free from the constant reminders. I wanted to move forward and not have my present and future stifled by my past. Room by room, I started to clean out the house. I made plenty of donations to thrift stores and sold some items online. When all was said and done, I had but a mere 20 percent left, but I still needed to downsize. This would have to come later. I knew the next step was to sell and move.

In August of 2021, I sold my house and moved into a newly built rental. It was a condo, and I was so happy to be free for the next chapter of my life. I only moved about eight miles, but it felt like worlds apart. The Lord opened the door, and I am grateful He did. I am so blessed and humbled that He saved and restored me.

I will say that my life is far from perfect, but the Lord has been so kind to me. I literally went from someone who borderline hated Christians to someone who deeply loves the body of Christ.

I will never minimize what I have experienced. My love for Joe as a spouse and friend was as real as any love can be outside of God's plan and hand. I say that because losing him was the hardest thing I have ever had to endure. The only comfort I have in his loss is that he is with Jesus. Satan lost both of us, and I am forever grateful to my Lord and Savior, Jesus Christ.

One saying I have used often and came to me while in prayer one day at the beginning of this journey was:

"I do not know what tomorrow holds, but I know who holds tomorrow."

> *"Therefore do not worry about tomorrow,*
> *for tomorrow will worry about its own things.*
> *Sufficient for the day is its own trouble."*

MATTHEW 6:34

Conclusion

IT HAS BEEN OVER THREE AND A HALF YEARS SINCE Joe passed, and my life has completely been changed through the power of His cross. I am now fifty-seven years old and am grateful on every level to my Lord and Savior, Jesus Christ, for redeeming me and giving me a reason to live. My life is now hidden with Him (Colossians 3:3). I will never forget Joe; we spent twenty years together. Joe and I were completely broken and without Christ for most of our lives. When I met him, I learned he was involved with the occult and had the ability to harness astral projection among other things. I, on the other hand, always looked for a man to provide protection for me. The wounds of my sexual abuse drove me to seek out this type of man. I was looking for safety because I was never afforded it when I needed it most. My abuse left me to fend for myself. This is why I was drawn to certain men. It fed my dysfunction and what had gone unmet. This world is a cruel place, but I am confident that God's grace and mercy will always triumph over judgement and this world.

I know what it is like to give your life to Jesus, walk away from Him, and yearn every moment just to be with Him. My life took a twenty-three-year detour because I bailed on

Him. He never did that to me. One of my favorite promises in the Bible is in Hebrews 13:5: "'I will never leave you nor forsake you.'" When God makes a promise, He does not and cannot go back on it. His Word, character, and motives are all pure, just, and motivated out of love.

If you are a Christian and feel discouraged, I understand your feelings, even though I may not have experienced your exact pain. I encourage you not to give up and walk away as I did. He will meet you where you are and take you where He wants you to be.

If you have read this book and do not yet know Jesus as your Lord and Savior, I am so happy that you have finished this book, not because I wrote it, but because I believe the Holy Spirit is drawing you close. Always remember, God loves you no matter what you have done or where you have been. There is no catch to His plan of redemption, but you must decide whether you will accept or reject Him. Nobody else can make that decision for you; only you can choose. He will never crash your door down, but He does stand at the door of your heart and knock.

"Behold, I stand at the door and knock.
If anyone hears My voice and opens the door,
I will come in to him and dine with him, and he with Me."

REVELATION 3:20

We have all heard of John 3:16, and this verse never loses truth despite the number of times it has been quoted. God's plan was never to keep a divide between Himself and His creation. Jesus became the sacrifice that would give us access to God and reestablish the line of communication between us and heaven. I love verse 17, but it is rarely quoted with verse 16.

For God so loved the world that He gave His only begotten Son, that whoever believes in Him should not perish but have everlasting life. For God did not send his Son into the world to condemn the world, but that the world through Him might be saved.

JOHN 3:16-17

Talk to God; ask Him to forgive you. Tell Him you want Him to come into your life and make you a new person. The person He intended you to be in Him. You can share everything with Him, and He will never reject you. I often talked to Jesus, even when I was not serving Him. It is kind of ironic, but I wanted to believe He loved me and cared even though it was a struggle.

I realize some are afraid of what they may have to give up before coming to Jesus. I will tell you what I gave up: sin, death, despair, loneliness, and hell. I have gained so much more: joy, peace, purpose, and heaven. The list of gains far outweighs the other. It will be for you as well because what God did for me, He will do for anyone. There is not a human alive who is able to clean themselves up before God will save them. He has already paid the price. Your ticket is paid for; you just need to claim it. I urge you to give your life to Him and find a church that can help you grow. He will lead you to where He wants you to be. Today is the day of salvation; tomorrow is not promised.

For He says: "In an acceptable time I have heard you,
And in the day of salvation I have helped you."
Behold, now is the accepted time;
behold, now is the day of salvation.

2 CORINTHIANS 6:2

This is my account, and I can say without hesitation that at the darkest part of my life, I had the most hope and peace.

In closing, God bless you and may He abundantly reveal His great love for you. Thank you for your time.

About the Author

GROWING UP IN NORTHEASTERN Ohio, Dan graduated high school in 1984 and enlisted in the US Air Force. Besides traveling the world, his time with the Air Force was well spent earning several degrees, including a BS in Occupational Education. None of the degrees naturally lead to the path of writing a book, yet he enjoyed the English classes he took while in college.

Throughout his life, God relentlessly pursued Dan, ultimately transforming him into a new person in Him (2 Corinthians 5:17). *And Such Were Some of You*, his first book, came from his desire to share his testimony with others. This life story chronicles the transformative process of God's deep love. The changes he has experienced are not behavior modification, or mind over matter. Jesus Christ has redeemed Dan, and he gives Him all the credit, glory, and praise. Dan's desire is for people to accept Jesus Christ as their Lord and Savior. If He can reach Dan (and He did), He can and will reach anyone.

Dan currently resides in the Columbus, Ohio, area, where he is an active member of his church and community. His parents still live in the Youngstown area, while his sister is rooted in Florida. He is single and looks forward to his life in Him. God bless you as you go through your life. May He reveal His great love for you in every area.

Made in the USA
Columbia, SC
14 February 2024

31561074R00057